...ng in the Forest 1-2-3

Aaron R. Murray

Enslow Elementary
an imprint of

Enslow Publishers, Inc.
40 Industrial Road
Box 398
Berkeley Heights, NJ 07922
USA

http://www.enslow.com

Enslow Elementary, an imprint of Enslow Publishers, Inc.

Enslow Elementary® is a registered trademark of Enslow Publishers, Inc.

Library of Congress Cataloging-in-Publication Data

Murray, Aaron R.
  Counting in the forest 1-2-3 / Aaron R. Murray.
      p. cm. — (All about counting in the biomes)
  Includes index.
  Summary: "Introduces pre-readers to simple concepts about the forest using short sentences and repetition of words"—Provided by publisher.
  ISBN 978-0-7660-4053-3
  1. Forest ecology—Juvenile literature. 2. Forest animals—Juvenile literature. 3. Counting—Juvenile literature.
I. Title. II. Title: Counting in the forest one-two-three.
  QH541.5.F6M88 2012
  577.3—dc23

                                        2011039556

Future editions:
Paperback ISBN 978-1-4644-0065-0
ePUB ISBN 978-1-4645-0972-8
PDF ISBN 978-1-4646-0972-5

Printed in the United States of America
032012 Lake Book Manufacturing, Inc., Melrose Park, IL
10 9 8 7 6 5 4 3 2 1

To Our Readers: We have done our best to make sure all Internet Addresses in this book were active and appropriate when we went to press. However, the author and the publisher have no control over and assume no liability for the material available on those Internet sites or on other Web sites they may link to. Any comments or suggestions can be sent by e-mail to comments@enslow.com or to the address on the back cover.

♻ Enslow Publishers, Inc., is committed to printing our books on recycled paper. The paper in every book contains 10% to 30% post-consumer waste (PCW). The cover board on the outside of each book contains 100% PCW. Our goal is to do our part to help young people and the environment too!

Photo Credits: © 2011 Photos.com, a division of Getty Images, pp. 1, 10, 16; iStockphoto.com: © lendry, p. 14, © Tomasz Kopalski, p. 3 (pinecone); Shutterstock.com, pp. 3 (blueberry, squirrel), 4, 6, 8, 12, 18, 20, 22.

Cover Photo: Shutterstock.com

Note to Parents and Teachers

Help pre-readers get a jumpstart on reading. These lively stories introduce simple concepts with repetition of words and short simple sentences. Photos and illustrations fill the pages with color and effectively enhance the text. Free Educator Guides are available for this series at www.enslow.com. Search for the *All About Counting in the Biomes* series name.

Contents

Words to Know

blueberries   pinecone   squirrel

Gray squirrel

Let's count!

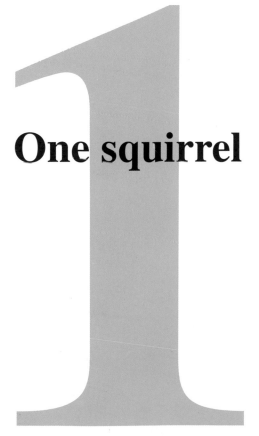

One squirrel

Raccoon

Two eyes

White-tailed deer

Three deer

Four wolves

Five eggs

Six blueberries

Seven pinecones

Eight leaves

Mallard ducks

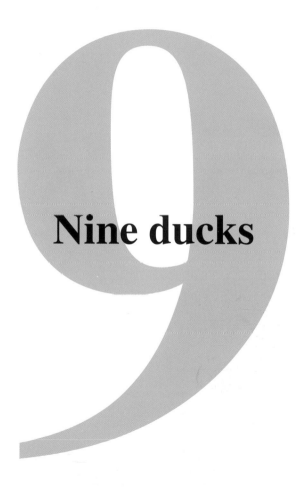

Nine ducks

Canada geese

Ten birds

Read More

Cefrey, Holly. *Coniferous Forests.* New York: Powerkids Press, 2003.

Guiberson, Brenda Z. *Life in the Boreal Forest.* New York: Henry Holt and Company, 2009.

Salas, Laura Purdie. *Temperate Deciduous Forests: Lands of Falling Leaves.* Mankato, Minn.: Picture Window Books, 2007.

Web Sites

Biomes of the World: Temperate Deciduous Forest
   <http://www.mbgnet.net/sets/temp/index.htm>

Kids Do Ecology: Temperate Forest
   <http://kids.nceas.ucsb.edu/biomes/temperateforest.html>

Index

Guided Reading Level: A
Guided Reading Leveling System is based on the guidelines
recommended by Fountas and Pinnell.

Word Count: 22